C0-BLE-973

Follow Your Dream

Nancy White

Fearon
Belmont, California

DOUBLE FASTBACK® ROMANCE Books

Chance of a Lifetime
Follow Your Dream
Good-Bye and Hello
Kiss and Make Up
Love in Bloom
A Love to Share
Never Too Late
No Secrets
The Road to Love
A Second Look

Cover illustrator: Terry Hoff

Copyright © 1987 by David S. Lake Publishers, 500 Harbor
Boulevard, Belmont, California 94002. All rights reserved.
No part of this book may be reproduced by any means,
transmitted, or translated into a machine language without
written permission from the publisher.

ISBN 0-8224-2383-9
Library of Congress Catalog Card Number: 86-81651
Printed in the United States of America
1. 9 8 7 6 5

"Hey, Mimi, what shift are you working today?" Lena asked, smiling at her co-worker.

Mimi brushed a few strands of long hair out of her dark eyes and sighed. "I'm on from three till eight," she said, making a face.

"What happened?" Lena asked eagerly. "I thought you had your acting class tonight."

Mimi frowned. Lena always had to ask a thousand questions. Sometimes it got on Mimi's nerves.

Mimi was determined to be an actress. That's why she only worked part-time as a word processor at Wordco Industries. She spent the rest of her time on auditions and acting classes. She also read everything she could about acting. At first she'd wanted to be a soap-opera star because they got to wear such pretty clothes. Then she'd decided she'd rather go after more meaning-ful roles. Mimi had dreamed of a serious acting career since she was 14 years old. She knew she would never let go of that.

Mimi snapped out of her daydream. "Yes, Lena, I do have class tonight," she sighed. "But I'm not going because Mrs. Mariner insisted that she needed me to work."

She could still hear Mrs. Mariner's words. "You're one of my best operators. I'm really counting on you. And you know that Rogers and Wells is one of our biggest clients."

Mrs. Mariner was always "counting on" Mimi. That was because there were only two things in Mrs. Mariner's world, Wordco and her husband, Robert. Or "Ro-Ro," as she called him. Mimi thought the nickname made him sound like a dog. Acting and entertainment were of no importance to Mrs. Mariner. Mimi tried to think of anyone else she knew who refused to own a television. Ro-Ro and MM, the office nickname for Mrs. Mariner, were the only ones.

Mimi shoved her huge shoulder bag into her desk drawer. "Working tonight is definitely a drag," she complained to Lena.

"How come MM asked you stay?" Lena persisted.

Mimi sometimes wondered if Lena ever said anything that wasn't a question.

"Because she's in love with Wordco," Mimi answered. "And acting is nothing but child's play in her eyes."

At last Lena seemed satisfied and turned back to her work. Soon Mimi was lost in her daydreams again. How she hated to miss tonight's class! She'd been scheduled to read one of the lead parts in a play the class was rehearsing. It was an honor to read a lead part, and she'd been practicing for days. She'd even redone her long hair into a stylish arrangement of waves on top of her head. It would have been perfect for the role.

But Mrs. Mariner had tracked her down and asked her to work. The request had seemed to carry a slight hint of a threat. And Mimi didn't want to chance losing her part-time job at Wordco. It was a great job to have until she finally made the grade as an actress. The hours were usually flexible, and the pay wasn't too bad. And it was a lot better than waiting on tables. All of her friends from acting class worked in restaurants to support themselves. Compared to that, Mimi had it pretty good.

Mrs. Mariner had left some work for Mimi to start on. Her heart sank as she looked at the stack of tapes. "Not depositions again!" she thought to herself. Some documents weren't too bad, but for some reason, she found depositions especially boring. Listening to hours and hours of people talking about a will or a car accident! It hadn't seemed so boring when she had first started as a word processor. But by now depositions were a real pain. Still, since she had to do them, she decided to make the best of it. She started to pretend that the tapes were the script of a play, and she took the part of one of the lawyers.

Soon Mimi became lost in her own world, typing the words of a Mr. William Krandall and dreaming of herself on stage. Then someone tapped her on the shoulder.

Startled, she snapped her head around and caught the wire of the earphones on her collar. She was angry at being taken away from the stage. But she immediately forgot her anger when she saw who had interrupted her. She tried not to stare at his curly dark hair and soft brown eyes as she took off her earphones. Anything this guy had to say might be worth coming back to the real world for.

"You look as if you were lost in another world," the man said to her, grinning. Mimi felt a little embarrassed. She hoped he wasn't making fun of her.

"I guess I was, in a way," she replied. Mimi thought he had one of the nicest smiles she had ever seen.

"I'm Jose Bionde," he said pleasantly. Then he placed 12 more tapes on her desk.

"Is that the way you introduce yourself to everyone?" she asked with a groan.

"It's my name," he answered innocently. "Don't you like it?"

"I didn't mean your name," Mimi said. She pointed to the tapes. "I meant those."

"They're out of my hands," he teased.

"I can see that," she replied. "They're right on my desk." She made a face at the tapes, then instantly regretted it. She didn't want Jose to think she was immature.

"Don't you like the Rogers and Wells depositions, Mimi?" he asked.

"How did you know that?" Mimi asked, startled.

"What—about the depositions or your name?" Jose asked, teasing again.

Mimi laughed. "Both, I guess," she replied.

"Well, nobody likes the Rogers and Wells stuff, except Mrs. Mariner, and . . ."

He paused and looked down for a second. "It was MM herself who told me your name."

All of a sudden Mimi realized that Jose was in a wheelchair. She'd thought he was sitting in the chair next to her desk. She tried not to stare at the spoked wheels and the chrome handles.

Jose caught her eye. "Didn't you know that I'm the *big wheel* around here?" he asked. He winked at her. "At least that's what my friends call me."

Mimi felt like hiding in one of her desk drawers. Why couldn't she keep her eyes off the wheelchair? "I . . . I'm sorry," she stammered.

"To tell you the truth, I am too," Jose said matter-of-factly. "About the accident I mean. It happened about three years ago. My legs were paralyzed in a diving accident at the city pool."

Mimi started to feel sorry for him. "Oh . . . ," she began softly.

Jose looked very serious. "I know. It's such a shame," he said. "You have no idea how hard it is to get up the ladder to the diving board in a wheelchair. And then I have to wheel out on the board and roll off the end as fast as I can." He shrugged his shoulders.

Mimi's mouth dropped open in horror. He was joking about it! She could only stare at him. But when his face brightened with that charming smile, she couldn't help but smile back. "That's terrible," she said. "You shouldn't joke about it."

"Why not?" Jose returned. "Who'd be better at teasing innocent young women like you?"

Mimi then realized that the wheelchair wasn't important. Wheelchair or not, Jose was one of the cutest and, she had to admit, one of the funniest guys she'd met in a long while.

"I'm not so innocent," she protested.

"Well, I know you can't be new here," Jose said. "Or MM wouldn't be trusting you with the Rogers stuff. How come I haven't seen you before?"

"I wonder how I could have missed *you*," Mimi responded, flirting a bit. Jose was so easy to talk to. "I don't usually work these hours," she continued. "And besides, I only work part-time. What shift do you usually work?"

"This one," he answered. "But not on a part-time basis. I work here from three till eleven, and I also have a job in the morning."

"You're kidding!" Mimi exclaimed. "What are you, a workaholic?"

"No. I just want to get ahead," Jose replied. His eyes took on a slightly deter-mined look. He looked the way Mimi felt when she talked about acting.

"What do you want to do?" she asked him.

"I'd like to own a setup like this, some-day," he said, gesturing around the office.

"Wow, that's getting ahead all right," Mimi said.

"How come you only work part-time?" Jose asked her.

"I'm part-time because I'm studying to be an actress," she answered. "I mean I *am* an actress," she corrected herself. "I take classes in drama, and I've had a few parts in community theater plays."

Jose gave her a serious look, as if he were really interested in what she was saying. "Isn't that kind of a risky profession?" he asked.

Mimi shrugged her shoulders. "I love it," she replied. "I'm willing to take chances to be able to act." Her eyes met his. "Isn't that the way you feel about your dreams?" she asked him.

12

"I don't know. Why don't we talk about it on our break?" he suggested.

His invitation was so casual and natural that Mimi couldn't think of anything she'd rather do. "Sure," she answered. "I'll meet you at the elevator at six-thirty."

"Fine. See you then," he said as he wheeled his chair away.

"**D**id you know that they use this coffee to clean the copy machine?" Jose teased. He held his nose as he raised the styrofoam cup to his mouth.

"I heard that they use it in the floor cleaner," Mimi replied, laughing.

The two of them sat at a corner table in the Wordco cafeteria. Daydreaming happily for a second, Mimi quickly brought her attention back to the conversation.

"Isn't acting a long, uphill road?" Jose was saying.

"What do you mean?" Mimi asked.

He ran his long fingers through his wavy hair and looked at her intently. Mimi felt an urge to reach over and touch his hair, but she squelched the feeling right away.

"Well," Jose continued, "it's not very stable, is it? You can work very hard without knowing if you'll ever be successful. I could never live like that." He paused. "How often do you really get a chance to perform?" he asked.

Mimi felt a little defensive about her acting dreams. "Why can't people understand how alive I feel when I'm acting?" she thought. "Why can't Jose understand?"

She tilted her head a little higher. "First of all," she said, "I get lots of chances to perform. Besides the community theater, we do cabaret shows and performances on the stage at the Sea Gull."

"That restaurant over on Eighth and Harper?" Jose asked. He looked surprised. "I didn't know they had drama."

Mimi smiled proudly. "Maybe if you weren't such a dedicated businessman you'd get out a little more," she kidded him. Then she poked him in the arm just to make sure he knew she was teasing.

Jose reached over and gave her hair a gentle tug. "Very funny," he said. "I'm not a millionaire yet. But if I keep working the way I am now, I may come close someday. I can't understand how you can get so involved in something so uncertain."

Mimi shrugged her shoulders. "You just don't understand how exciting it is to be another person," she replied.

"What do you mean?" Jose asked, looking puzzled.

Mimi gestured, her hands waving through the air as she tried to describe what acting was like. "It's as if you actually become another person," she began. "You live another person's life for a short time. You experience that person's happiness, sorrow, dreams . . ." Her voice trailed off and she looked at Jose, wishing she could make him understand.

He smiled at her sweetly. "I can't pretend I understand a hundred percent. But I'll tell you one thing. I don't think *you* have to pretend to be anyone else. You're perfect just as you are."

Mimi felt herself blush. She swallowed some of her coffee, which had grown cold. "I'm not perfect," she murmured. Then she glanced at her watch just so she wouldn't have to look into Jose's eyes. "Oh, no," she exclaimed. "Look what time it is!"

Jose quickly checked his watch. "I don't believe it," he cried. "We've been here half an hour! I thought we'd only been gone about ten minutes."

"MM is absolutely going to kill me," Mimi wailed. "She's already warned me twice about socializing on company time. I have to get back to my desk."

Jose groaned. "Now do you understand why I want to be my own boss someday?" he asked. "So that people like MM can't tell me what time to come and go. What time to have coffee, when I can talk to people . . ."

"Jose," Mimi cut in, "we're not going to have jobs at all if we don't get back right now."

Mrs. Mariner was there just as they got to the door of the cafeteria. She flashed them a sharklike grin. "I was wondering where you two were," she said, a little too sweetly. "How are you coming along on the Rogers and Wells depositions, Mimi?"

"We were just discussing them, Mrs. Mariner," Mimi lied, trying to look sincere. She thought that only MM would believe that she and Jose would discuss something as boring as the Rogers and Wells depositions on their coffee break.

Mrs. Mariner looked pleased. She must have actually believed Mimi. "Well, that's good," she replied. "But you really should be *doing* them, not just talking about them."

Jose gave Mimi a look of disbelief. Mrs. Mariner turned and quickly walked away.

"I can't believe you told her that with a straight face," Jose said when Mrs. Mariner was out of earshot.

"And you think that acting is silly," Mimi answered with a smile. "It comes in handy on a lot of occasions."

Jose snapped his fingers and abruptly changed the subject. "I almost forgot," he said. "I'm having a party this Saturday night. Can you come?"

Mimi's acting skills came in handy once again. She pretended not to be as excited as she felt. "I'd love to," she answered with only half the enthusiasm that was welling up inside her.

"I'm just having a few old friends over," Jose said with a grin. "It would be fun to have a new friend come, too. But something in his eyes told her that she might become more than just a friend to him.

O
n Saturday night, Mimi had no trouble finding Jose's apartment building. She'd read the directions so many times she'd memorized them. Jose lived in an older part of town. Some people called his neighborhood rundown, but Mimi thought it was interesting and colorful. She parked her car in a space right in front and walked up the steps to a large wooden door. Taking a deep breath, she entered the building.

Mimi looked at the directions in her hand as she got on the elevator. It was a good thing she'd memorized them. She'd been so nervous driving over that she'd crumpled the paper into a tiny ball. Now she could barely read Jose's apartment number.

When she reached the sixth floor, there was no need to search for the right apartment. She just followed the sounds of laughter and music to a door halfway down the hall. Taking another deep breath, she knocked quietly on the door. A blond woman opened it and motioned her in.

Mimi took a quick look around and realized that she didn't know a single person in the room. She hadn't expected to see a lot of familiar faces. But she'd thought at least a few people from work might be there. Instead she saw about 20 strangers crowded into Jose's small living room.

"What a terrific sweater," the blond commented in a friendly voice.

Mimi was pleased. This was the first time she had worn the black sweater covered with sparkling silver and gold stars. She had been worried that it might be too flashy. She smiled gratefully at the woman. "Gee, thanks, I—" she began.

"Here you are," a familiar voice cut in. Mimi turned to see Jose wheeling his chair up next to her.

"Didn't I tell you she was a star?" Jose said proudly to the blond woman. "Just look at that sweater."

"I'm sorry. I don't believe we've met," Mimi said politely to the woman.

"I'm sorry," Jose apologized. "I should have introduced you. This is my neighbor, Joanne," he said to Mimi.

Joanne smiled. "You must be Mimi," she said.

"You knew that because she's the only stranger in the room," Jose pointed out.

Joanne gave Jose a meaningful glance. She then turned to Mimi and said, "I know because I've been hearing about you all week."

Mimi was surprised. "If only I could talk to her alone for a few minutes," she thought. "I wonder what Jose has been saying."

Jose frowned at Joanne, pretending to be mad. "What a loyal friend," he said dryly. "Really knows how to keep a secret. Come on, Mimi. Let me introduce you to my *real* friends." He winked at Joanne. "And you'd better go check on Larry in the kitchen," he said to her. "He seemed very interested in something Maria was saying a few minutes ago."

"He'd better not be *too* interested," Joanne laughed. Then she turned to Mimi. "It was good to meet you," she said warmly. "And don't worry. Jose's only said good things about you." With that, she left them and walked toward the kitchen.

Later, Mimi was sitting on the couch telling one of Jose's friends about her acting classes. She looked up to see Jose wheeling toward them. "I know it's Saturday night, Luis," he said to his friend. "But isn't it getting a little late?"

Mimi thought she heard a faint note of jealousy in Jose's voice. It made her feel even more hopeful about him. He must really like her if he cared enough to be jealous.

Luis checked his watch. "Sorry, pal," he apologized. "I didn't realize what time it was." He smiled approvingly at Mimi. "Talking to you sure made the time go fast," he said as he got up to leave.

"So, what do you think of my friends?" Jose asked Mimi when Luis was gone. He took her hand.

"They're terrific," she answered. Then she paused. "Can I tell you a secret?" she asked.

"You can tell me anything," Jose answered softly.

"I was terribly nervous before I came here tonight," Mimi confessed. "But everyone was so friendly that I felt comfortable almost at once."

"They all liked you," Jose told her. He squeezed her hand and then looked straight into her eyes. "Can I tell *you* a secret?" he asked.

"Of course," Mimi answered. She longed to hear any secrets Jose would tell her.

"I think I'm falling in love with you," he replied. The way he said it was so simple and direct that the words went straight to Mimi's heart.

"I think that's the nicest secret I've ever heard," she whispered.

Jose leaned closer to her. "I know a better way of telling secrets," he said softly. He took her face in his hands and gently kissed her forehead. Then he moved his mouth down to her waiting lips.

"What's going on, Mimi? Why do you look so happy?" Lena asked curiously.

Mimi had been feeling so good the past few weeks that she hadn't even minded Lena's questions. She and Jose were getting to know each other very well. He had become her best friend, and their love was growing every day.

Of course, they had their differences. Jose placed great importance on being stable and secure. Mimi wasn't exactly irresponsible. She knew that acting wasn't secure. But she was willing to live with that in order to follow her dream. And she didn't mind Jose's desire for stability. In fact, it made her feel secure with him.

"Mimi, where are you?" Lena called out jokingly. Mimi had become lost in her thoughts again.

Mimi laughed. "Sorry, Lena," she said.

"How come you look so happy?" Lena repeated.

"Well, first of all, there's Jose," Mimi began. She had shared some of her feelings about her new boyfriend with Lena. "And then there's the play."

"What play?" Lena wanted to know.

"I told you about it," Mimi said. "It's the one I'm auditioning for at the community theater."

"What's it about?" Lena asked.

Mimi rolled her eyes. Sometimes she thought Lena would be happier working for the CIA or some other organization where she could ask people questions all day long. "Remember?" she asked. "It's a romantic comedy called *Dreams Can Come True*."

Lena nodded.

Then Mimi put her headphones on. She was still working on material for Rogers and Wells. It seemed as if they never stopped taking depositions from people. She continued to think about Jose while she listened to a voice on the tape. The voice droned on about being cheated out of some money by an ungrateful nephew.

The next day was Mimi's second audition for a part in *Dreams Can Come True*. When the director called her back for a second reading, she'd hardly been able to keep from dancing around her apartment. "I have a chance!" she'd said to herself. "They wouldn't be calling me back unless they thought I did a good job."

She began to wonder what part they'd ask her to read for. Of course, she dreamed of landing the lead part. But she figured that because she was young and inexperienced, she'd be given a small part to read.

It would probably be Rachel, a woman who comes to a party, says a few funny lines, and is never heard from again. Still, the part was a good one. And Mimi believed the old saying that there were no small parts, only small actresses. "If I'm lucky enough to get any part," she thought, "I'll give it all I've got."

She looked in the mirror one last time. Her acting teacher had told her that jeans would be too casual for the audition. She hoped the royal blue slacks with the white shirt would be OK. She had left the top two buttons of the shirt undone and loosely tied a black and white striped tie under the collar. "It'll have to do," she thought as she turned from the mirror.

Just then the phone rang. Mimi hoped that the producer's office wasn't calling to postpone the audition.

"Hello," she said nervously as she answered.

"Hi," Jose said brightly.

"Oh, I'm so glad it's you," Mimi sighed with relief.

"You'll really be glad when you hear the news," he said excitedly. "I was able to get tickets to a Firebirds concert."

"You're kidding!" Mimi exclaimed. "They've been sold out for months. How did you do it?"

"My brother-in-law works at the Civic Auditorium. He got tickets for me," Jose told her happily.

"Which night are the tickets for?" Mimi asked. She knew that the Firebirds were putting on several shows. They were one of the most popular groups in the country.

"They're for Friday night at eight," he answered.

"Oh, no," Mimi groaned, her heart sinking. "Friday's the night of the final audition for the play."

"So audition another night," Jose said impatiently.

"You know it doesn't work that way," Mimi protested. "You have to audition when they ask you to."

"What kind of audition would be held on a Friday night, anyway?" Jose's voice was rising with anger. "Do you have to go?" He sounded hurt, too.

Mimi felt guilty confessing the truth. "Well, the second audition is this afternoon," she admitted. "I don't know yet if they'll call me back for the final audition Friday."

"Are you kidding?" Jose demanded angrily. "You're turning me down when you're not even sure you'll have to be there?"

"I can't take the chance," Mimi said in a pleading voice. "Why can't you understand how important this is? Why do you always seem to think your dreams are more important than mine?"

"Who's talking about dreams?" Jose shot back. "I'm asking you to a concert that everyone in town wants to see. And some-how I had the idea that *I* was important to you."

Mimi felt herself growing angry. "That isn't fair," she objected. "You *are* important to me. But so is acting. Can't I have both? Do I have to be available to you 24 hours a day?" Her words sounded harsher than she had intended. But at that point she was almost too angry to care.

"I didn't deserve that," he answered.

"I'll show you," Mimi declared. "Someday you'll be dying to see *me* onstage instead of some rock group!" She slammed down the phone.

Mimi was not going to let Jose's phone call ruin her chances at the audition. In fact, their argument made her more determined than ever to do her very best.

Somehow her anger helped her to feel more confident as she entered the theater. She walked right up to one of the producer's assistants and told him her name.

He handed her a script with some pages clipped together. "Here," he said, "look over the lines for Rachel's part. You'll be reading in about half an hour."

"Rachel. Just as I thought," she said to herself. She went backstage and found an empty chair. She knew the play backwards and forwards, but she went over Rachel's lines one more time.

"Mimi Consolo! Out front, please," she heard an assistant call.

Mimi stood up quickly. Then she walked onto the stage and gave one of the best readings she'd ever done.

"Would you please step down front, Ms. Consolo?" a voice from the darkened audience called.

Mimi moved toward the front of the stage. She shaded her eyes against the stage lights, but she couldn't really see who was talking to her.

"That was quite a reading," the voice said.

"Thank you," Mimi responded. She wished she could see who was speaking. An assistant? The producer? The director?

"Please come back on Friday for another reading," the voice spoke again.

She could hardly believe it! They were asking her back for the final audition. She was one step closer to her dream.

When Mimi got home, she wanted to call Jose and tell him her wonderful news. She was still angry, but not nearly as much as before. But she figured it was too late to call him. And after their phone call earlier, she was a little scared. The good news would just have to wait.

By Friday night, Mimi felt drained. She was nervous about the audition, and she still hadn't talked to Jose. "Oh, well," she thought. "If tonight goes well, maybe I'll have even better news for him. He'll *have* to be happy for me if I get a part in the play."

She got to the theater half an hour early and went directly backstage. Sitting alone in a corner, she thumbed through her well-worn script. She decided she could read any part in the play. By now, she knew them all by heart.

Deep in concentration, Mimi heard a voice say, "Hello." Looking up, she saw a cute guy with light brown hair pulling a chair up next to her.

Mimi gave him a faint smile. "Hi," she responded.

"Nervous?" the guy asked in a friendly voice.

"A little," Mimi answered. She ran her fingers through her hair and laughed. "No, a lot," she admitted.

"I guess I am, too," he said. "I'm Paul Morton. I'll be reading for Mark."

"Wow, the lead," Mimi said, impressed. "No wonder you're nervous. I'm Mimi Consolo. I'm reading for Rachel's part, which means we won't have any scenes together."

"That's a good part, though," Paul reassured her. Mimi liked his friendly, easygoing manner.

Just then, an assistant came back to check on things. "Everyone all set?" he asked the various actors and actresses scattered around the huge backstage area. A few of them nodded.

He came over to Mimi and Paul. "All set for Mark?" he asked Paul.

"I'll give it my best," Paul answered casually, showing none of the nervousness he'd just confessed to Mimi.

"And how about you," the assistant asked, looking at Mimi. "Got Karen's part down?"

"Karen?" Mimi gasped. "That's the lead. I . . . I thought I was reading for Rachel."

"Who told you that?" the assistant asked, dismissing her question with a wave of his hand.

"I thought that because I read for her part last time," Mimi explained.

The assistant shook his head. "That's the last straw," he said angrily. "I told my

secretary to call everyone. She was supposed to confirm your readings. Didn't she
get to you?"

"No," Mimi gulped.

"That's it," the assistant said. "She goes. I
can't put up with any more of her mixups."
He paused for a second. "You know Karen's
part, don't you?" he asked her.

Mimi took a deep breath. "Sure," she said,
as confidently as she could.

"Great," the assistant said as he walked
away.

Mimi turned to Paul. "I can't believe it,"
she said in amazement. "I thought I was up
for the role of Rachel. I haven't rehearsed
for Karen's part. I mean I have, but not as
much as I would have liked to. I mean . . ."
She laughed. "I've got to stop babbling."

"Would you like to go over the lines now?" Paul asked.

"That'd be terrific," Mimi said gratefully.

The two went over a few scenes together while some of the other people auditioned. Mimi felt as if she and Paul were becoming friends. One of the things she loved about the acting field was the way actors and actresses became friends so quickly. They all seemed to have so much in common.

Mimi found herself telling Paul about Jose. She confided how much she cared about him. She also described how hard it was to make Jose understand that acting was more to her than just a little hobby.

"No matter what he thinks, you've got to continue with what you believe in," Paul assured her. "You won't be happy any other way. And," he added, "Jose probably wouldn't respect you much if you weren't doing what you really wanted."

"Paul! Mimi! You're on," a voice called to them from beyond the stage.

"Good luck," they whispered to each other.

Afterward, Mimi and Paul stood backstage discussing the audition.

"I shouldn't have come in so quickly on that last line," Mimi said in frustration.

"No, that was OK," Paul reassured her. "But how about the way I stumbled over the word 'investigate'? I'm glad this show is supposed to be a comedy. I wanted to disappear through the floorboards when I did that."

"How long do you think it will take them to make up their minds?" Mimi wondered.

"Probably not too long," Paul answered. "But it'll seem like years to us." He was trying to look calm, but Mimi could hear his voice trembling a bit.

Then Mimi blurted out nervously, "I don't know if I can stand this! Does pursuing an acting career mean it's going to be like this for another 30 years? Just waiting to see if one dream after another comes true? This is awful!" She gave a sigh and then corrected herself. "No, it isn't," she said wearily. "I was so happy out there on stage, acting Karen's part, becoming Karen. I'll go through all the waiting in the world if I have to."

Just when Mimi had calmed down, the assistant came backstage.

"Will the following people please stay," the assistant requested in a bored voice.

He began to read names at random. Mimi couldn't tell when—or if—her name would come up. That made the suspense even worse.

"Paul Morton," the assistant called. Mimi reached over and hugged Paul. "Congratulations!" she said, thrilled for him. She was so excited that she almost didn't hear her own name being called.

Paul hugged her back. "Isn't this great?" he exclaimed.

The assistant finished reading the list, then dismissed those whose names hadn't been called. Mimi stole a quick glance at the actors who hadn't been given parts. She felt a stab of sympathy for them. It really could be painful pursuing a dream to act. But tonight was her night. She had gotten the part!

Mimi was working at Wordco that Saturday afternoon. Another big job from Rogers and Wells had come in, and Mrs. Mariner had begged her to help out. Since she needed the money, she quickly agreed.

She had wanted to call Jose the night before to tell him about getting the lead. But she figured he'd be at the concert, and she was awfully tired when she got home. Besides, she knew that she'd see him at Wordco. He worked just about every Saturday.

Mimi sat at her word processor working on another deposition. "No, I never saw any car go through the red light," the tired-sounding voice on the tape was saying. Suddenly, she felt a tap on her shoulder.

She turned around and saw Jose sitting there in his chair. Instantly she realized how glad she was to see him.

"I wanted to call you last night," she said to him with a smile. "But I was too tired to stay up. And I knew you'd be out late because of the concert."

Jose didn't return her smile, although he didn't seem angry either. "I didn't go to the concert," he said, looking down at his hands.

Mimi was shocked. "You what? Why not?" she asked in surprise. She knew how much he'd wanted to go.

Jose looked embarrassed. He shrugged his shoulders and mumbled, "I didn't feel like going without you." Then he looked up. "How did the audition go?" he asked.

"I got the lead!" Mimi exclaimed, glad for the chance to tell him the news. "I'm going to star in the play. Well, I'm not the only star," she corrected herself. "This guy I met named Paul is going to be the other star."

"That's nice," Jose said. He didn't look very excited.

"Is that all you can say?" Mimi asked. She felt sort of let down. "Don't you realize what this means to me?"

"I know what it means to *me*," Jose said. "It means we'll have less time than ever together. And it's acting, Mimi. It's not the real world." He sighed. "How much will you get paid for your time?" he asked.

"You know it's a community theater," Mimi said. "We don't get paid anything but expenses. I was afraid that you'd respond this way. I even told Paul how you felt about the whole thing."

Jose looked furious. "So you talked to this guy about me," he said angrily. "And he's an actor, so he probably understands you better than I do, right? Maybe you should go out with him tonight instead of me."

Mimi poked Jose playfully. She didn't like the way he was acting. But it was hard to be mad at him when he was jealous. "Don't be silly," she said lightly, hoping he'd respond to her casual manner. "There are two reasons we have to go out tonight. We have to continue this fight, and we *always* go out on Saturday. It's as simple as that, right?"

Jose relaxed a little and managed a small grin. "You win," he said. "I'll see you tonight." He leaned over and gave her a light kiss on the cheek. "And congratulations," he added. Then he started to leave, but quickly stopped. "I almost forgot," he apologized. "Mrs. Mariner told me she wanted to see you in her office."

"What does she want?" Mimi asked.

"I have no idea," Jose said with a shrug. "She just said it was important."

Mimi sighed. "I might as well get it over with," she said. "I'll see you later."

"I'm so glad to see you," Mrs. Mariner greeted Mimi as she walked into her office. "I have something very exciting to tell you."

Mimi doubted that, but she tried to look as interested as possible.

Mrs. Mariner cleared her throat. "As I'm sure you're aware," she began, "we've been getting a lot of extra work from our clients recently. And it looks as if it's likely to continue." She looked expectantly at Mimi.

Mimi realized that she was supposed to say something, but she didn't know how to respond. "That's really nice," she said politely. She realized that this must mean a lot to MM.

"It's more than just nice," Mrs. Mariner pointed out. "It's a wonderful opportunity for you. I'm able to offer you a full-time position as supervisor of our special accounts," Mrs. Mariner announced, her smile broadening.

Mimi was stunned. She knew she had been a good worker. But she didn't think she was the supervisor type, especially at a place like Wordco. Not wanting to hurt MM's feelings, she put her acting abilities to use once again. "That's a very flattering offer," she said, hoping she sounded sincere. "But I'm going to have to think about it for a little while. It would mean a big change for me."

"All right," Mrs. Mariner said, "but I'm going to need an answer by Monday." She seemed to be disappointed that Mimi wasn't dancing around her office for joy.

"I'll have an answer by then," Mimi assured her. "And thank you for the offer." She left the office and walked back to her word processor.

Later that evening, Mimi and Jose sat eating dinner at a nearby pizza parlor. Mimi had just told Jose of MM's offer.

"What did you say to her?" Jose asked.

"I told her I'd give her my answer on Monday," Mimi replied. "I'm not sure that would be the best job for me."

Jose frowned. "I can't believe you didn't grab the opportunity," he said. "It's a great chance to get ahead. Doesn't the security of a good job mean anything to you?"

"You care enough about security for both of us, don't you think?" Mimi asked. "Why can't you understand that acting is my *real* profession? My job at Wordco is just a sideline."

"Well, it's the sideline that pays your rent, not your acting," Jose pointed out. His eyes looked sad. "If you took the job and cut down on acting, we'd see each other more often."

"We'll still see each other," Mimi said softly. "Do you think that because of the play I'm going to give up the leading man in my real life?"

"It sounds as if the leading man in your life is going to be that Paul guy," Jose said with a frown.

Mimi started to get a little impatient. "I told you he's just a friend," she said.

"Yeah, and how much friendlier will you be after rehearsing together for weeks?" Jose asked bitterly.

"Oh, I don't want to talk about it any-more," Mimi said in a weary voice. Jose was sounding a little too jealous right now. "I wonder if you'll ever be able to under-stand how happy I am when I'm acting," she sighed.

Jose shook his head. "I think you're making a big mistake turning down the promotion," he said. "I also think you're making a big mistake about the two of us. You say we'll have enough time together, but we won't. You care more about acting than you do about me. And you're going to have to make a sacrifice somewhere."

"Don't say that, Jose. It's so unfair," Mimi protested. "This should be a *happy* night."

She and Jose should have been celebrating her success, not fighting. "If this is what the future together is going to be like," she thought, "it looks pretty grim."

Jose turned out to be right about one thing. Mimi's rehearsals took up most of her time. But he had been wrong when he said she'd regret her decision. Mimi was happier than ever. If she could have seen Jose a little more often, she wouldn't have minded if rehearsals went on 24 hours a day.

Of course, she still had her part-time job at Wordco. She had politely told Mrs. Mariner that she just wasn't the right person for the supervisor's job.

Finally the opening night of the play arrived. Mimi had been asked to work a few hours at Wordco that day. At first she had been upset, but by now it seemed like a blessing in disguise. Concentrating on work helped keep her from being so nervous.

She hadn't seen Jose yet, but Lena said that he was around. Mimi left a ticket for the performance on his desk.

The dress rehearsal the day before had been thrilling. But when it came time for the performance that night, Mimi was ten times as excited.

Just before the play was to start, Mimi peeked through the curtain and looked for Jose. Then a voice called, "Places, everyone!" and Mimi had to draw back from the curtain.

She went over to Paul, who was standing farther back on the stage. "I can't see him," she wailed. "I don't even know if he's here."

Paul gave her a friendly hug. "Don't worry," he said. "No one can see into the audience from the stage." He laughed. "Maybe it's just as well. This way you won't be so nervous."

Paul walked over to his place on the stage, and Mimi and the other actors followed. Within seconds, the curtain rose, the audience applauded, and the play began.

During intermission, Mimi again looked for Jose in the audience. She still couldn't see him. "Did he even see the ticket?" she wondered. "Is he still mad?"

And yet, this was turning into one of the happiest nights of Mimi's life. The audience applauded in the right places and laughed at the funny lines. Mimi felt right at home on stage. Still, the one thing that would have made it complete would have been knowing that Jose was out there watching. Maybe then he'd have understood.

The second act went even better than the first. And when the final curtain came down—after two curtain calls and a standing ovation from the audience—the cast assembled backstage for a party.

"A toast to the stars!" cried one member of the cast as she held up her glass.

"I heard that some agents from New York were in the audience," someone else said.

"To Broadway!" everyone cheered as they raised their glasses with a feeling of triumph.

Mimi's heart leapt into her throat. She had caught sight of Jose. He was wheeling toward her with a single red rose in his lap.

Mimi hugged him as soon as he reached her. "I'm so glad you're here," she whispered in his ear. "I was thinking of you the whole time I was onstage."

Jose handed her the rose. "Is there someplace we can have some privacy?" he asked.

"Sure, come on back to the dressing-room area," she answered. "Everyone'll be out here celebrating for quite a while."

When they were alone, Mimi sat next to Jose. She rested her head on his shoulder while he stroked her hair. "I've been so blind," he said to her. "Seeing you tonight, seeing all the magic you created and how happy you looked . . . I understand now that you were right about your acting."

Mimi turned her face toward him, and he gave her a soft, gentle kiss. As she snuggled up to him she whispered, "Now *all* my dreams have come true."